MW01129249

Ethan's Story:

My Life With Autism

Written By Ethan Rice

Illustrated by Crystal Ord

Published by Anchor Group

Copyright 2012 Dannett Rice
Published by Anchor Group
Edited by Melissa Ringsted
Illustrated by Crystal Ord
Author Photo by Photography by Kyla
ISBN: 978-0-9855385-2-1

This book is dedicated to everyone with autism.

All kids are different. They are all different sizes.

I am tall.

They have different color eyes.

Mine are bright blue.

Some have special needs like eating a special diet or wearing glasses. For me, my brain works differently-

I have autism.

#7 SCHOOL BUS

I see the world in a different way.
It is hard for me to make friends. I don't always
understand how children play together. I like it
when there are set rules of what to do.

When I talk to people, it is hard for me to look them in the eye.

It makes me a little scared to do that.

I am more comfortable not looking at people when I talk. Sometimes I don't know that someone is talking to me if they don't get my attention first.

I get very nervous when things change. I like things to be the same and for everything to happen on schedule.

I get extra excited when I am looking forward to something happening, like a holiday or special event.

Sometimes when I get excited or anxious, I get extra wiggly and I have a hard time sitting still. Running, jumping, and tight squeeze hugs help me to calm down inside.

I also have a vest I can wear when I get nervous that feels like a big hug.

Sometimes I lose track of where my body is and I run into people. I don't mean to and I really don't like fighting.

When there is fighting,
I try to get away -
fighting is no fun
for me.

Sudden movements may scare me
and I do not really like surprises.

My autism makes some things easier for me.

I am really good at math and reading
and I know all of my states and capitals.
I also love "I Spy" and hidden pictures
and doing number games with
my grandparents.

Autism is so very, very fun. I like how school is easy for me. I like getting big hugs. And I like having autism because...

...this is
the way God made me!

It might be hard for me to make friends,
but when I do I'm a very good friend.
Now that you know what autism is-

- Who wants to be my friend?

About the Author

Ethan Rice is eight years old and lives with his family in Michigan. He is the oldest of five children. He enjoys math and reading, playing basketball and flag football, and being a Cub Scout. When he grows up Ethan wants to be a farmer, and he wants the whole world to know that Jesus loves them.

94650076R00018

Made in the USA
Columbia, SC
28 April 2018